D1270044

FITZROVIA:
LONDON'S BOHEMIA

Michael Bakewell

NPG

Published in Great Britain by National Portrait Gallery Publications,
National Portrait Gallery, St Martin's Place, London WC2H 0HE

ISBN 1 85514 256 2

A catalogue record for this book is available from the British Library

Series Project Editors: Celia Jones and Lucy Clark
Series Picture Researcher: Susie Foster
Series Designer: Karen Stafford
Map of Fitzrovia by Advanced Illustration
Printed by Clifford Press Ltd, Coventry

Front cover
Nancy Cunard, 1896–1965
Cecil Beaton, late 1920s (detail)
Bromide print, 24.1 x 18.8 cm
© Courtesy Sotheby's, London
National Portrait Gallery (x40077)

For a complete catalogue of current publications,
please write to the address above.

CONTENTS

❧

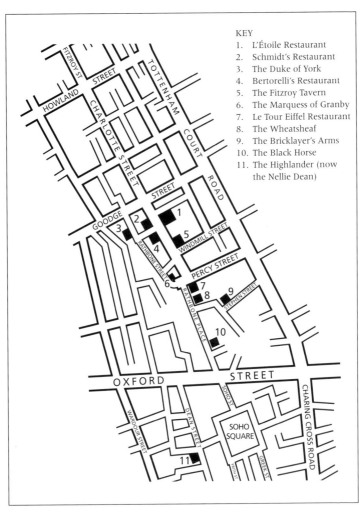

KEY

1. L'Étoile Restaurant
2. Schmidt's Restaurant
3. The Duke of York
4. Bertorelli's Restaurant
5. The Fitzroy Tavern
6. The Marquess of Granby
7. Le Tour Eiffel Restaurant
8. The Wheatsheaf
9. The Bricklayer's Arms
10. The Black Horse
11. The Highlander (now the Nellie Dean)

Map of Fitzrovia (based on Ruthven Todd's *Fitzrovia: Part of Soho*)

INTRODUCTION

A ny account of Fitzrovia must inevitably be tinged with nostalgia, with memories of smoke-filled bars awash with anecdote, of untidy larger-than-life monologists keeping watch on their half-empty glasses out of the corner of their eye, exuberant, vainglorious and self-aggrandising, relentlessly haranguing their listeners like ancient mariners while deadlines passed disregarded and commissions were left in the lurch. Much of the story of Fitzrovia is of talent blighted, promise unfulfilled and premature death through drink.

Fitzrovia, for much of the first half of the twentieth century, was London's Bohemia. The district had been the meeting-place of artists since the eighteenth century. The sculptor Joseph Nollekens lived there as did the painter Fuseli. Richard Wilson, the landscape painter, and John

HENRY FUSELI,
James Northcote,
1778

5

JOHN CONSTABLE,
self-portrait, *c.*1804

Constable both had studios there. Edwin Landseer was born in the area as was Dante Gabriel Rossetti. It was here that Arthur Rimbaud and Paul Verlaine came in 1872 seeking refuge in the 'flat black bug' of London.

The golden age of Fitzrovia, although such a term is barely appropriate, spanned a period from the mid-twenties until the end of the Second World War. Many of the characters who spent their lotus-land existence in its pubs and clubs are now half forgotten: the art critic Tommy Earp, the poet Ruthven Todd, and Jack Lindsay, founder of the Fanfrolico Press. 'We were babies who prattled ourselves into worlds of great achievement . . .' remembered the writer Philip O'Connor in his autobiography, 'the charms of the district were those of minimal effort, of paddling in sensations wafted in by the busy proper people surrounding our encampment.'

The district is bordered by the Euston Road in the north and Oxford Street in the south, with Portland Place and Tottenham Court Road as its western and eastern limits. Its main artery begins as Fitzroy Street, crosses Howland Street to become Charlotte Street and, at the junction with Percy Street, turns adroitly into Rathbone Place.

Although only the narrow line of Tottenham Court Road divided Fitzrovia from Bloomsbury, the two were worlds apart. Bloomsbury was almost universally regarded by the Bohemians as affected and effete. Constant Lambert once described a dream he had in which Anthony Powell went up to Virginia Woolf at a party, greeting her with, 'How now, bluestocking, what about the booze?'

Fitzrovia prided itself on being down-to-earth, no-nonsense, sturdily professional. It was essentially a pub culture, fuelled by drink and conversation, with none of the uniformity of outlook that characterised Bloomsbury. There was no Fitzrovian ethic and no Fitzrovian philosophy. The two worlds did, of course, frequently overlap. Roger Fry, one of Bloomsbury's icons, founded the Omega Workshops in Fitzroy Street and was the lover of the 'Queen of Bohemia', Nina Hamnett. Walter Sickert moved freely between the two societies, as did Augustus John, who was Ottoline Morrell's lover.

The Fitzroy Tavern, Charles Allchild, 1930s

The journalist and politician Tom Driberg is generally credited with giving the area its name, after the Fitzroy Tavern, a solid Victorian

Drinking at the Fitzroy Tavern (Betty May is second from the left), unknown photographer, 1930s

pub on the corner of Charlotte and Windmill Streets, whose landlord in the twenties and early thirties was the massive Judah Kleinfeld. The Fitzroy, likened to a station bar at rush-hour, was the meeting-place of the London Bohemians, although it was very far from being exclusively an artists' pub. Poets and painters would find themselves rubbing shoulders with a colourful collection of local characters, including Albert Pierrepoint, the last public hangman, Prince Monolulu, the peacock-plumed bookie, the black-magician Aleister Crowley and whole boat-loads of visiting sailors.

In the mid-thirties Kleinfeld retired, leaving the Fitzroy in the hands of his daughter Annie and her husband Charles Allchild. The pub became something of a tourist attraction, partly on account of its celebrated clientele but also because of its charity work for children, financed by donations speared on darts and thrown at the ceiling. Some of the regulars decided that the fun-fair atmosphere was becoming too much for them and decided to emigrate a few hundred yards south to the pubs christened by Anthony Burgess the 'Maclaren-Ross Circuit', after the latter's definitive account in his *Memoirs of the Forties*.

Each of these pubs had its own folklore. The Black Horse, where the circuit began, a little way up Rathbone Place from Oxford Street, was generally judged 'too funereal to be convivial', and one of its landlords had reputedly drunk himself to death. A little further along, set back in Gresse Street, stood the Bricklayers Arms, known to the Fitzrovians as the 'Burglars' Rest' after a gang of thieves broke in and spent the night there, leaving behind them a formidable quantity of empties.

Next came the Wheatsheaf, where a small elderly lady called Mrs Stewart arrived promptly every evening at opening time to settle down with her bottle of Guinness and the crossword puzzle. According to Julian Maclaren-Ross, whose permanent post was at the corner of the bar next to her leather-bound bench, 'great care had to be exercised in offering her a drink'.

Across the road from the Wheatsheaf stood the Marquess of Granby where, Maclaren-Ross wrote, 'gigantic guardsmen went in search of homosexuals to beat up and rob', and where a man was once battered to death on the pavement. Further up Rathbone Street stood the Duke of York, patronised by the less reputable Bohemians and from which Maclaren-Ross was barred by the manager, Major 'Alf' Klein, the 'Prince of Goodfellows'.

The Fitzrovians' drinking pattern was regulated by highly eccentric licensing laws. The Fitzroy and the Wheatsheaf were both in the Borough of Holborn and closed at 10.30 p.m., whereas the Marquess of Granby was in Marylebone and stayed open until eleven. Every night at 10.30 there would be a stampede to the places which remained open, and frequently the company at the Wheatsheaf would rush down Rathbone Place and across Oxford Street to the Highlander in Dean Street, a pub much favoured by the film-making fraternity, and now known as the Nellie Dean.

To be a Fitzrovian did not mean that one had to live there. To Dylan Thomas, surging in from Wales or to the Scots poet W. S. Graham arriving from the north, the pubs of Charlotte Street and Rathbone Place offered a second home, a place where they felt instinctively on their own ground. Fitzrovia belonged as much to them as it did to Nina Hamnett, the enduring symbol of London's Bohemia.

The Second World War provided Fitzrovia's finest hour, with the black-out, the shortage of almost everything, and the very real danger of the air raids giving an added feeling of excitement to the nightly drinking ritual and heightening the sense of camaraderie. After the war Fitzrovia began slowly to disintegrate. The film industry, which had kept many writers and composers in work, could no longer support them; some, like Constant Lambert and Dylan Thomas, met early deaths, others drifted away to the country. For those that remained, Broadcasting House still offered a means of survival and the walking wounded of Fitzrovia deserted the Wheatsheaf and the Fitzroy for the pubs patronised by the BBC Features Department, the Stag and the George. When the department was dissolved in 1964 much of the old spirit of Fitzrovia expired with it.

Now only the pubs remain with their photographs and press cuttings of a vanished past. Soho, with its tougher, more abrasive, but equally alcohol-fuelled, culture, became Fitzrovia's heir and its successor.

SELECT BIBLIOGRAPHY

Gordon Bowker, *Pursued by Furies: A Life of Malcolm Lowry*, Harper Collins, 1993.

Anthony Burgess, *Little Wilson and Big God*, Heinemann, 1987.

Arthur Calder-Marshall, *The Magic of my Youth*, Hart Davis, 1951.

Anne Chisholm, *Nancy Cunard*, Sidgwick & Jackson, 1979.

Dan Davin, *Closing Times*, Oxford University Press, 1975.

Paul Ferris, *Dylan Thomas*, Hodder & Stoughton, 1977.

Sally Fiber, *The Fitzroy*, Temple House Books, 1995.

Constantine Fitzgibbon, *The Life of Dylan Thomas*, Dent, 1965.

Victoria Glendinning, *Edith Sitwell*, Weidenfeld & Nicolson, 1981.

Cecil Gray, *Musical Chairs*, Home & Van Thal, 1948.

Nina Hamnett, *Laughing Torso*, Constable, 1932.

Nina Hamnett, *Is She a Lady?*, Allan Wingate, 1955.

Michael Holroyd, *Augustus John*, Chatto & Windus, 1996.

Denise Hooker, *Nina Hamnett: Queen of Bohemia*, Constable, 1986.

Justine Hopkins, *Michael Ayrton*, Andre Deutsch, 1994.

Augustus John, *Chiaroscuro*, Jonathan Cape, 1954.

Augustus John, *Finishing Touches*, Jonathan Cape, 1964.

Percy Wyndham Lewis, *Blasting and Bombardiering*, Eyre & Spottiswood, 1937.

Jack Lindsay, *Fanfrolico and After*, Bodley Head, 1962.

Julian Maclaren-Ross, *Memoirs of the Forties*, Alan Ross, 1965.

Andrew Motion, *The Lamberts*, Chatto & Windus, 1986.

John Pearson, *Façades*, Macmillan, 1978.

Anthony Powell, *To Keep the Ball Rolling*, 12 vols., Heinemann, 1976–82.

Edith Sitwell, *Taken Care Of*, Hutchinson, 1965.

Osbert Sitwell, *Noble Essences*, Macmillan, 1950.

Derek Stanford, *Inside the Forties*, Sidgwick & Jackson, 1977.

John Symonds, *The Great Beast*, Macdonald, 1971.

WALTER SICKERT (1860–1942)

If the subject of a picture could be stated in words there had been no need to paint it. (Walter Sickert, *The Language of Art: The New Age*, 1910.)

From the mid-1900s until the end of the First World War, Sickert had a studio in Fitzroy Street which served as the headquarters of the Camden Town Group of painters and as the setting for his celebrated Saturday afternoon at-homes. He was one of the first Fitzrovians, though he cannot be tied exclusively to one place. He had been born in Munich; his father was of Danish descent, his mother Anglo-Irish; he spent much of his life in Dieppe, yet he was inescapably English. 'He guarded the English tradition, which he had to rescue from the hands of the mediocre,' wrote Osbert Sitwell, 'with something of the growling adroitness with which a lion guards a bone.'

WALTER SICKERT, Philip Wilson Steer, before 1894

Sickert's studio had once belonged to James McNeil Whistler for whom he had briefly worked, but Whistler's influence had been rejected in favour of his own very personal style and subject matter, dark but richly coloured studies of seedy, claustrophobic interiors peopled with bored and faded men and women.

Not that there was anything seedy or faded about Sickert himself. He was a dandy and something of a wit. 'As a talker he could hold his own with Whistler and Wilde', wrote the painter William Rothenstein, 'yet he preferred the exhausted air of the music-hall, the sanded floor of the public house, and the ways and talk of the cockney girls who sat to him.'

He had begun life as an actor, playing small roles in Henry Irving's company, and to the end of his life one of his famous party tricks was to recite long stretches of *Hamlet*, play-ing all the parts. It may have been his early years on the stage which stimulated his curiously protean nature. Wilson Steer's portrait painted before 1894 shows him at his most formally elegant but on other occasions, as Nina Hamnett observed, 'he might appear with an enormous beard like a Crimean vet-eran [as in the sketch by Kapp] or he would dress himself in very loud checks and a bowler hat and look like something off a race-course.'

Nina Hamnett, who posed for Sickert, met him at one of his famous Fitzroy Street afternoons. Guests approached the crowded studio through corridors clad in tin and glass, which reminded Osbert Sitwell of the *Cabinet of Doctor Cali-gari*. The assembly was by no means wholly Fitzrovian. Arnold Bennett

WALTER SICKERT, Edmond Xavier Kapp, 1940

came, as did William Walton, W. H. Davies, the poet and professional tramp, Aldous Huxley and Percy Wyndham Lewis. Conversation would range from the identity of Jack the Ripper (Sickert claimed to know it) to Degas and the 'carnival reputation' of Matisse. When conversation flagged there were always the unending absurdities of the Irish writer George Moore.

Sickert was a person of unusual charm, but he could be mischievous and even malicious. At a Sitwell dinner party he approached Wyndham Lewis and announced, 'I give you this cigar because I so greatly admire your writing', but promptly deflated Lewis by adding, 'If I liked your paintings I'd give you an even bigger one.'

He was one of the few who were equally at home in both Fitzrovia and Bloomsbury. Virginia Woolf, who described him as a 'rusty rat-trap with hard little eyes', considered him the 'greatest English painter living'. For her, his paintings were novels without words, a sentiment that apparently pleased him.

NINA HAMNETT (1890–1956)

Nina Hamnett was Fitzrovia's most notorious inhabitant, the 'queen of Bohemia', a living legend, part of the furniture of the Fitzroy Tavern, which she never deserted. 'To enter Kleinfeld's and not to buy Nina a drink,' wrote the novelist and biographer Constantine Fitzgibbon, 'was in those days and in that world, a solecism that amounted to a social stigma.' She would repay the courtesy with an anecdote. She had been everywhere and known everyone. A painter of considerable promise, she had studied at the Slade School of Art and had been encouraged by Augustus John and Sickert (who made a number of nude sketches of her). When Roger Fry set

NINA HAMNETT, Walter Sickert, *c.*1916

up the Omega Workshops in Fitzroy Street in 1913, Nina was one of the first recruits. She subsequently became his mistress: 'the most fascinating, exciting, tantalising, elusive, beautiful, exasperating creature in the world.'

At the Allied Artists Exhibition that same year she encountered the sculptor Henri Gaudier-Brzeska. They became lovers: he made a figure of her dancing naked (Nina was much given to dancing naked) and two marble torsos. 'You know me, m'dear – I'm in the V and A with me left tit knocked off!' was how Nina introduced herself to the young poet Ruthven Todd. This was the *Laughing Torso* which provided her with the title for her autobiography.

In 1914 she took a room opposite the Café de Dôme in Montparnasse and became a close friend of Modigliani. She met Picasso and Erik Satie, Francis Picabia and the young novelist Raymond Radiguet. She is said to have entertained Diaghilev, Stravinsky and Cocteau with a rendering of 'She was poor but she was honest' and sang sea-shanties to Rudolph Valentino.

All this time Nina continued to paint but she turned, almost exclusively, to portraits: 'I am more interested in human beings than landscapes and still lives.' Her sitters included the Sitwells, Francis Poulenc, Lytton Strachey and W. H. Davies.

She returned to London in 1926 and it was from this time that she became a regular fixture at the Fitzroy, bringing with her, according to the music critic Cecil Gray, 'a nostalgic breath of the old spirit of Montparnasse'. Nina had always been a drinker but now she began to lose her ability to cope with it. She was also beginning to develop a taste for the 'rough trade', and the Fitzroy was always a haven for boxers and sailors. Asked why she always had such a soft spot for sailors, she replied 'Because they leave in the morning'.

After the war Nina lost most of her old allure and panache and presented rather a pathetic picture, as in Daniel Farson's photograph, shabby, smelling of drink and rather short of teeth. She had outlived her time, although she did manage to produce a rather disjointed second volume of her autobiography, *Is She a Lady?* In December 1956 she heard a broadcast of a radio play *It's Long Past the Time* by her old friend, Robert Pocock. It was intended

NINA HAMNETT, Daniel Farson, 1952

as an affectionate portrait but Nina saw it as a grotesque caricature. Convinced that she had been deserted by all her friends she threw herself, or drunkenly fell, from her balcony and was impaled on the railings below.

AUGUSTUS JOHN (1878–1961)

AUGUSTUS JOHN, Sir William Orpen, exhibited 1900

Augustus John entered Fitzrovia, as did so many others, by way of the Slade School of Art on the other side of the Tottenham Court Road. Like Nina Hamnett, he came from Tenby, in South Wales, and he was expected to study for the Bar. Eventually his family decided that 'Art might be just the thing for me, since it involved irregular hours, few social obligations and no arithmetic'. At the Slade, around the time of Orpen's portrait, John acquired a legendary reputation as the artist who would prove the finest draughtsman since Michelangelo. Wyndham Lewis said he was 'a great man of action into whose hands the fairies stuck a brush instead of a sword'.

In 1897 he moved into a first-floor flat in Fitzroy Street where he was joined by his sister Gwen. 'We shared rooms together, subsisting like monkeys, on a diet of fruit and nuts.' The Slade was noted for its 'talented and highly ornamental girl students' and John lost no time in marrying one of them, the beautiful Ida Nettleship, who had been kissed in her nursery by Robert Browning. They moved into a top-floor flat at 95 Fitzroy Street.

John began to cultivate the radically Bohemian appearance that was to make him the most instantly recognisable artist in Britain – long hair,

'abundant growth of virgin beard', a wide-brimmed hat, a black silk scarf secured by a silver brooch, earrings borrowed from the gypsies he loved to paint and whose nomadic life style he was determined to imitate.

He bought a caravan and was rarely able to resist the 'call of the road'. Nor was he able to resist the many women who came into his life. In 1903 he fell passionately in love with Dorelia McNeil,

AUGUSTUS JOHN, ?John Hope-Johnson, n.d.

LADY OTTOLINE MORRELL, Augustus John, 1919

'whose smile opens infinite vistas to me', and Ida was obliged to accept her as part of the John ménage. The relationship somehow managed to survive innumerable love affairs – with Ottoline Morrell, 'one doesn't meet Ottolines every day', with the Marchesa Casati, 'a spoilt child of a woman', and with many others. The affairs with Ottoline and the Marchesa at least resulted in striking and memorable portraits.

As he grew older, portraits began to dominate John's output. They guaranteed him a steady income and all the leading personalities of the day sat to him: Thomas Hardy, W. B. Yeats, James Joyce, George Bernard Shaw, Dylan Thomas, generals and admirals, city fathers and society beauties. His sitters were not always happy with the result. Gerald du Maurier said that John's portrait of him would 'drive me either to suicide or strong drink'.

Augustus John, Bill Brandt, before 1946

John had many homes, in Chelsea, in Martigues, in Cornwall, but he always returned to Fitzrovia to drink double rum and brandy at the Fitzroy Tavern or to dine his friends at the Tour Eiffel in Percy Street, where he would set up his headquarters.

John established himself as the most famous artist in England, yet for all his success, there was a general feeling that he had never lived up to the awe-inspiring promise of his early years. The art critic Anthony Blunt wrote in the *Spectator* in May 1938, 'Everyone is agreed on the fact that Augustus John was born with a quite exceptional talent for painting – some even use the word genius – and almost everyone is agreed that he has in some way wasted it.'

PERCY WYNDHAM LEWIS (1882–1957)

I will go into my credentials. I am an artist – if that is a credential.
I am a novelist, painter, sculptor, philosopher, draughtsman, critic,
politician, journalist, essayist, pamphleteer, all rolled into one, like one
of those portmanteau-men of the Italian Renaissance.

(Percy Wyndham Lewis, *Blasting and Bombardiering*, 1937)

Lewis was born in Nova Scotia but came to England as a child. He studied at the Slade and had a brief flirtation with the Omega Workshops, but quarrelled with Roger Fry – quarrelling was something of a speciality with Lewis – and parted company.

It was from Lewis's studio in Fitzroy Street that in 1914, with Ezra Pound, he launched *Blast*, bright puce in colour, 12 by 9$^1/_2$ inches, the organ of the Vorticist movement. Vorticism – the word was coined by Pound but the movement itself was largely Lewis's invention – drew on Futurism and Cubism 'attracting everything to itself, absorbing all that is around it into a violent whirling – a violent central engulfing'.

Lewis was the movement's leader and prophet, and the author of its manifestos:

Our Vortex rushes out like an angry dog at your Impressionistic fuss.
Our Vortex is white and abstract with its red hot swiftness.

Among the targets at which the 'angry dog' rushed out were the 'futurist' poet Marinetti, Thomas Beecham, 'sentimental gallic gush', the Bishop of London and the English sense of humour:

BLAST HUMOUR
Quack ENGLISH *drug for stupidity and sleepiness.*

Lewis's painting was a reflection of his combative personality: vigorous, vertiginous, as if spat out by an angry machine, with frenzied automata and angular scaffolding. Even his portraits (and this self-portrait) managed to suggest that his subjects were being relentlessly transmogrified by some metallic process.

PERCY WYNDHAM LEWIS, self-portrait, 1932

Percy Wyndham Lewis, Michael Ayrton, 1955

Lewis was a brilliant, pyrotechnic conversationalist, a natural leader, aggressive and contumacious, skilled in the art of making enemies. Cecil Gray found his appearance equally formidable:

Whatever the season of the year, whatever the prevailing climatic conditions, he would invariably be enveloped in a large dark overcoat with the collar turned up, a large black sombrero with the brim turned down, and gloves, so that practically all one saw of his person was a pair of eyes which peered out, through formidable horn-rimmed spectacles upon a hostile world . . .

(Cecil Gray, *Musical Chairs*, 1948)

In his novel *The Apes of God* (1930), Lewis launched a ferocious and brilliantly funny attack on Bloomsbury in general and the Sitwells in particular, who were pilloried as Lord Osmund, Lord Phoebus and Lady Harriet Finnian Shaw, 'God's Peterpaniest family'. Originally he had been one of their supporters and had attended the first performance of *Façade*. He had painted a portrait of Edith (now in the Tate Gallery) but, after they quarrelled, left it unfinished, depriving her of her hands, which she considered one of her finest features.

'Poor man!' she wrote in her autobiography, 'The only real fault in him was an unconquerable suspicion of anyone who admired his great potential gifts, seeing in that admiration a plot to gain his confidence and then hand him over to his real or imaginary enemies.'

In his later years Wyndham Lewis went blind, as he is shown in Michael Ayrton's portrait, but he worked on until his death on his novel sequence *The Human Age*.

DYLAN THOMAS (1914–53)

Dylan Thomas's first encounter with Fitzrovia was oblique but decisive. At the age of nineteen he was working as a very junior reporter on the *South Wales Evening Post*, 'making my daily call at the mortuaries – there's a lot of suicide in Wales.' In an article entitled 'Genius and Madness Akin in World of Art' he referred to Nina Hamnett as 'the author of the banned book *Laughing Torso*' and, for good measure, implied that she was insane. Her publishers threatened legal action and the paper was obliged to print an apology. Thomas was soon looking for another job.

When he began to make regular forays upon 'smoky London paved with poems', it was towards Fitzrovia that he generally directed his faltering feet for what he called his doses of 'the capital punishment', after which he would return to Wales, exhausted by 'too much talk, too much drink, too many girls'. The 'Rimbaud of Cwmdonkin Drive' began to cultivate a new personality and a new image. He became the 'Toughish Boy, the Boy with a Load o' Beer', caught by Michael Ayrton in his portrait – a marked contrast to the fresh-faced youth seen opposite. He rapidly established himself as an essential component of the Fitzrovian scene and his talk became legendary:

> *Gwilym begins: with the first pint a tall*
> *Story froths over, demons from the hills*
> *Concacchinate in the toilet, a silver ball*
>
> *Jumps up and down in his beer till laughter spills*
> *Us out to another bar followed by frogs*
> *And auks and porpentines and armadills.*
>
> (Louis Macneice, 'Autumn Sequel', 1954)

Dylan Thomas charmed Edith Sitwell: 'the first time I saw him I felt as if Rubens had taken it into his hands to paint a youthful Silenus,' and she became his champion. 'I could not name any poet of this, the younger generation, who shows so great a promise and even so great an achievement.'

Augustus John, who painted his portrait in *c*.1937–8, was less enthusiastic. He had been introduced to Thomas by Nina Hamnett at the Fitzroy.

Dylan Thomas, Augustus John, *c.*1937–8

DYLAN THOMAS, Michael Ayrton, 1945

At first he was amused: 'If you could have substituted an ice for the glass of beer you might have mistaken him for a schoolboy on the spree.' But he soon wearied of what he called 'the interminable reverberation of the alcoholic'.

Part of the reason for John's dislike was that Thomas had stolen Caitlin Macnamara from him, the daughter of an old friend whom he had taken under his wing. True to his reputation as a 'Casanova Ogre' John had made love to her. She called it rape and said he was an 'old goat'. John introduced her to Thomas at the Wheatsheaf where, Caitlin said, 'he put his head on my knee and never stopped talking.' According to legend they immediately took a room round the corner at the Tour Eiffel, where they stayed making love for several days, all of which was charged to John's account. They married in 1937.

Thomas established a formidable reputation as an apocalyptic surrealist with poems that were widely praised and imitated, even if, as in the case of the 'Ballad of the Long-Legged Bait' (1941), they were not altogether understood. At the same time he produced verse of enduring popularity – 'Fern Hill' (1946), 'In Country Sleep' (1947), 'Do not go Gentle Into That Good Night' (1951). He was, and still is, one of the few poets that the public could instantly recognise.

During the Second World War Thomas had a regular job, turning out scripts for propaganda films – 'Our Country', 'These are the Men', but when the war ended it was to the BBC that he turned for support. As his reputation as a poet grew the talk and the drink steadily took hold and the poems grew fewer and fewer. He became increasingly unreliable, taking advances for projects which were never fulfilled. The BBC were bombarded with increasingly desperate demands: 'ADVANCE IMMEDIATELY . . . I owe every tradesman in town.'

Poetry tours of America provided a temporary solution. They paid well, even though he brought none of the money home and the USA became a transatlantic Fitzrovia where the drink and the company and the talk absolved him of the need to write. One commission he did fulfil – largely owing to the tenacity of his producer, Douglas Cleverdon – was *Under Milk Wood*, which he handed over in October 1953. Augustus John hated it: 'The whole hotch-potch is a humourless travesty of popular life and is served in a bowl of cold cawl in which large gobbets of false sentiment are embedded. Pouah!'

BETTY MAY (1901–58)

'Betty May is, as you probably know, an artist's model', wrote Dylan Thomas to his old friend the poet and grocer Bert Trick in November 1934, 'who posed, though that is not perhaps the most correct word, for John, Epstein and the rest of the racketeers . . . I am going to write an article for her, under her name, for the *News of the World*. My payment will not be monetary, but, although she is not now as young as she was, that will not matter.'

Betty was Nina Hamnett's only rival in the Fitzroy and Nina kept a wary eye on her. Legend had it that she had been brought up in a Paris brothel, but another account situated her childhood in Limehouse. She had danced in *cafés chantants* in Bordeaux, had lived with the leader of an apache gang in Paris where she had a knife fight with her rival, earning herself the name of Tigre. Her (ghosted) memoirs were entitled *Tiger Woman* (1924).

She was a tiny, graceful woman with the face of an angel and ferocious green eyes. Arthur Calder-Marshall once encountered her coming out of a hotel in Museum Gardens, followed by five men: 'She was conspicuously dressed in a coat of tigerskin with a cap to match. With breeches, top-boots and a whip I could have fancied her putting a troupe of large cats through their routine, so masterful was her manner.'

At the Fitzroy, if the mood took her, Betty would squat down on all fours and lap up drink from a saucer. Her other party piece, which she performed in a basement club in Fitzroy Street called Wally's, was to sing 'The Raggle-taggle Gypsies' while taking off her skirt and waving it like a matador's cloak. She had many lovers, including the poet Jack Lindsay, and Douglas Burton, who was later found guilty of murder. She sold the story of their affair to the popular press.

In her twenties she had, like Nina Hamnett, been considerably involved with Aleister Crowley. She had married one of his devotees, a young Oxford undergraduate named Raoul Loveday, and had gone out with him to Crowley's abbey at Cefalù where Loveday died – of malaria, according to Crowley, but Betty believed that his death had been caused by the Master forcing him to drink the blood of a sacrificed cat.

When Nina Hamnett, who sketched Betty May at the bar of the Fitzroy, wrote her autobiography *Laughing Torso*, she included many anecdotes about Crowley, referred to Loveday's death and mentioned that

Crowley was 'supposed to practise Black Magic' on Cefalù. Rather misguidedly, Crowley took it into his head to sue her for libel. Nina called Betty May as her star witness and the popular press had a field day. Mr Justice Swift said that he had 'never heard such dreadful and horrible, blasphemous and abominable stuff as that which has been produced by a man who describes himself as the greatest living poet.' Predictably, Crowley lost.

Under cross-examination Betty May had told the court that passages in *Laughing Torso* had been ghosted: this was not well received by Nina. Some time afterwards

BETTY MAY, Nina Hamnett, n.d.

when a newspaper published a photograph of Betty May with a caption identifying it as Nina Hamnett, Nina took a cab down to the paper's offices and protested that she had been libelled. She was given £25 to pacify her. Returning to the Fitzroy to celebrate she thrust a glass of whisky into Betty May's hand. As soon as Betty May discovered the reason for this unexpected act of generosity she too descended on Fleet Street, and she too was given £25.

CONSTANT LAMBERT (1905–51)

CONSTANT LAMBERT, Christopher Wood, 1926

Christopher Wood painted his portrait of a slim, nervous, sensitive Constant Lambert in 1926. Behind Lambert's left shoulder there is a strategically placed bottle of gin, an unfortunate omen.

The two men had been brought together when Diaghilev, reckoning that a work by a young British composer might ensure financial backing for his London season, commissioned Lambert to write the music for a Romeo and Juliet ballet and Wood to design the decor and costumes. Lambert was already making a name for himself both as a composer and conductor and had demonstrated his ballet credentials with *Mr Bear-Squash-You-All-Flat*, based on a Russian fairy tale.

When Lambert arrived at Monte Carlo for rehearsals he found that Diaghilev had rejected Wood's designs and handed over the task to 'two tenth rate painters from an *imbecile group called the surrealists*' (Joan Miró and Max Ernst) and was taking an exceptionally free hand with Nijinskaya's choreography. He tried to withdraw the score but failed. When the ballet received its London premiere, a modest riot, led by Louis Aragon and André Breton, ensured its success.

Lambert scored his first public triumph in 1928 with 'The Rio Grande', a setting of a poem by Sacheverell Sitwell. He was a close friend of the Sitwells and was one of the speakers in *Façade* when it was performed at the Chenil Galleries in 1926.

In 1928 Lambert took a room in the bookshop run by the 'beautiful and stormy' Dorothy Varda in High Holborn, technically in Bloomsbury territory but close enough to the Fitzroy Tavern for Lambert to become a regular drinker there. Lambert loved talk and good company and drink. He was a great raconteur and a noted wit, famous for his bawdy ecclesiastical limericks. 'Lambert was prodigal of wit,' wrote Anthony Powell, 'he never dreamt of postponing a joke because the assembled company was not sufficiently important for a witticism to be used on it.'

It was Ninette de Valois who, seeing Lambert as 'our only hope of an English Diaghilev', brought him into the English ballet revival. He was appointed conductor and musical director of the Camargo Society, which eventually became the Sadlers Wells Ballet. His marriage to the exotically beautiful Florence Chater had run aground after the birth of his son and he became increasingly involved with the company's brilliant young dancer, Margot Fonteyn. In January 1938 he commemorated their love in *Horoscope* in which star-crossed lovers are eventually united.

Lambert's most ambitious work, *Summer's Last Will and Testament*, a setting of Thomas Nashe's 'pleasant comedy' of plague and death, was first performed in January 1936. His friend Michael Ayrton remembered, 'Constant felt such sympathy for Tom Nashe that this long dead Elizabethan practically joined the company of Constant, Cecil Gray, Dylan Thomas and myself when we went drinking round the town'.

Margot Fonteyn in *Horoscope*, Gordon Anthony, 1938

There was something compulsively self-destructive about Lambert's drinking which increasingly began to take its toll. In 1947 he married the painter Isabel Delmer, conveniently forgetting to inform Margot Fonteyn. Since they were both, in the choreographer Frederick Ashton's words, 'terrific topers', this did nothing to halt his downward alcoholic spiral. His decline was further aggravated by the fact that, unknown to himself, he was suffering from diabetes.

In July 1951 *Tiresias*, an hour-long ballet with Fonteyn in the lead, was performed before the Queen. It was an almost total disaster. 'Idiotic and boring' was the ballet critic Richard Buckle's comment. Lambert, inevitably, sought consolation in drink, and collapsed and died on 21 August 1951.

ALAN RAWSTHORNE (1905–71)

R awsthorne was born in the same year as Constant Lambert and was one of the closest friends of his last years. Lambert once drunkenly but sincerely proclaimed him 'the best young composer in England'. He was one of the 'extra pens' – Elizabeth Lutyens, Humphrey Searle and Gordon Jacob were the others – who worked under the direction of an exhausted Lambert on the orchestration of *Tiresias* so that the ill-omened ballet could meet its deadline. After the composer's death, Rawsthorne wrote his *Improvisations on a Theme by Constant Lambert* (1960), the theme being taken from the opening of *Tiresias*. It was dedicated to Lambert's widow, Isabel, whom he married three years later.

Isabel had designed the sets and costumes for *Tiresias* and was a painter of some repute. She had known André Derain, who painted her portrait, and was the model for one of Jacob Epstein's most memorable busts. Her work was considerably influenced by Giacometti, as her painting of Rawsthorne shows.

ALAN RAWSTHORNE, Isabel Rawsthorne, 1966

Rawsthorne was a northerner, born in Haslingden, Yorkshire. His parents were resolutely against his taking up music as a profession and he trained as a dentist and studied architecture before they eventually let him have his way. He shared Lambert's dislike of the English folk-music tradition and favoured a harder, grittier style that owed a good deal to Hindemith.

He settled in London in 1935, marrying the violinist Jessie Hinchliffe, and scored his first major public success with his *Symphonic Variations* four years later. Rawsthorne's house was one of the early casualties of the War and he lost most of his manuscripts but, undeterred, he started work on a violin concerto. Wartime service intervened, and when the concerto was eventually completed Rawsthorne penned a characteristically laconic note for its first performance: 'The interruptions thus occasioned by being successively blown up and called up have caused a considerable time to elapse between the initial stages of the work and its completion in 1947.'

ALAN RAWSTHORNE, Cecil Beaton, 1948

Rawsthorne was a witty talker, but never attempted to rival Lambert. He was a stylish dresser, as Beaton's photograph demonstrates, but not in the Maclaren-Ross manner. He was reticent and fundamentally deeply serious and never allowed good company and good drink to get in the way of his work.

ERNEST JOHN MOERAN (1894–1950)

Annie Kleinfeld, the daughter of the proprietor of the Fitzroy, had an autograph book to which the regulars were invited to contribute a poem, or a sketch, or, in the case of a composer, a musical fragment. On 16 November 1928, E. J. Moeran, generally known as 'Jack', wrote down a few bars of his 'First Rhapsody', and added 'you must find some words for this tune.' A year earlier, Constant Lambert had contributed a few bars from his ballet *Pomona*, and the following year Philip Heseltine (Peter Warlock) provided a scrap of his song 'Sally is Gone That Was so Pretty'.

Unlike Lambert, Moeran was fascinated by folk-music. His father had been Vicar of Heston in Norfolk and in company with Heseltine he had toured the Norfolk countryside in search of folk song. Heseltine, the model for Coleman in Aldous Huxley's *Antic Hay* (1923), had a distinctly sinister reputation; he had dabbled in the occult and declared Aleister Crowley to be 'by far the greatest living artist in England'. The composer Herbert Howells regarded him as Moeran's evil genius: 'one of the gentlest, nicest people God ever made, and a very promising composer . . . then he got in with the Heseltine clan, took to drink – you couldn't belong to that sort of unofficial club without it – and just went to the dogs.' The

An excerpt from 'First Rhapsody', Ernest John Moeran, 1928

gentle, sensitive aspect of Moeran is borne out by Augustus John's sketch and Howard Coster's more formal photograph.

Moeran had served in the Norfolk Regiment in the First World War and been badly injured. A scrap of shrapnel, lodged in his skull, made him particularly vulnerable to alcohol, something of a handicap for a friend of Heseltine, a regular at the Fitzroy and the lover of Nina Hamnett.

By the time he was thirty Moeran had achieved more than either Delius or Elgar at that age, but in 1926 he suffered a crisis of self-confidence. He abandoned work on a symphony commissioned by Hamilton

ERNEST JOHN MOERAN, Augustus John, *c*.1927

Harty, the conductor of the Hallé Orchestra, and gave up composing altogether. 'I nearly became a garage proprietor', he wrote, 'I had an awfully lazy period in Eynsford.'

Eynsford was a village in Kent where Moeran and Heseltine shared a cottage and where a motley collection of poets and artists and composers, including Lambert, Jack Lindsay and Nina Hamnett descended upon them, turning the place into a pastoral Fitzrovia. Lambert and Moeran performed their party piece, a spectacular and absurd Victorian piano duet entitled 'The Fairy Queen', constantly edging one another off the piano stool. On one celebrated occasion when a girl was evicted from her cottage, the clan turned out in full force to stage a demonstration in

ERNEST JOHN MOERAN, Howard Coster, 1944

her support, with Nina clad in a sheet and wearing a death's-head mask, Lambert in a beard and false nose and Heseltine in an enormous black hat that had once belonged to Augustus John. They continued their protest until the arrival of a troop of mounted police.

Eventually Moeran escaped to Ireland where he began work again. His father was of Irish descent and Moeran was very conscious of his Irish heritage. According to Nina Hamnett, when the pianist Harriet Cohen protested about the rough, discordant writing of passages in his piano concerto, he told her 'It represents Saturday night in a four-ale bar in County Kerry. Of course there are discords.'

MICHAEL AYRTON (1921–75)

From 1943 to 1952 Ayrton lived on the edge of Fitzrovia at All Soul's Place, close to Broadcasting House and to the George, one of Fitzrovia's outposts. Like Wyndham Lewis, whom he greatly admired, Ayrton prided himself on his breadth of talents: painter, sculptor, illustrator, poet, novelist, maze-maker, mythologist, occultist and a member of the BBC *Brains Trust*. 'An amazingly varied man', commented the novelist Mary Renault.

Ayrton's painting is generally categorised as 'Neo-Romantic', along with that of his friends, John Minton, John Craxton, Keith Vaughan and the two Roberts, Colquhoun and MacBryde. But towards the end of the forties he rejected Neo-Romanticism as being 'dangerously fashionable' and chose to follow a course directed by his own obsessive mythologies – St Anthony, Orpheus, Icarus and Daedalus, the Minotaur. In his exploration of classical legend he found a way both of examining himself and of mirroring his own time.

In his early years Ayrton was notorious for a certain belligerent and uncompromising arrogance. John Gielgud, for whom he was designing the set and costumes for a production of *Macbeth* in 1941, warned him against his 'ungraciousness of manner and lack of charm'. Ayrton did not suffer fools gladly and took pleasure in stirring up controversy. His celebrated onslaught on Picasso in 1945 – 'a vast erection of bones in the graveyard of expression' – prompted Colquhoun to denounce him as 'positively the enemy of painting'.

Unlike John Minton, Ayrton tended to steer clear of the more 'landlocked' Fitzrovians. He was happy to sit drinking with a fuddled Augustus John, he joined Dylan Thomas in a Hogarthian boat trip down the Thames (ending, inevitably, in the poet falling overboard), but although an enthusiastic drinker he drew back from the alcoholic abyss.

His closest friendship was with Constant Lambert, whom he met in 1943. They shared an ability to look at life 'as at once a profundity, a mystery and a huge joke'. The following year, Lambert moved in with him at All Soul's Place. The ballet was one of Ayrton's great passions and his friendship with Lambert gave him the opportunity to design decor and costumes for Albert Roussel's *Le Festin de l'Araignée* at Sadlers Wells, and for the controversially extravagant production of Purcell's *The Fairy*

Queen at Covent Garden. When the administrator, David Webster, alarmed by Lambert's drinking, decided to replace him with Karl Rankl, it was Ayrton who led the whole company to threaten to withdraw from the production, unless Lambert was reinstated.

In the early fifties Ayrton put London behind him and, with his new wife Elizabeth, went to live at Bradfields, a fifteenth-century farmhouse in Essex. His range of activities grew steadily wider, a film on Leonardo da Vinci with music by Alan Rawsthorne, portraits of Wyndham Lewis, Graham Sutherland and Henry Moore, a 'sculptural biography' of Hector Berlioz and, in the Catskills, a vast maze with figures of Daedalus and the Minotaur at its centre.

MICHAEL AYRTON, self-portrait, 1947

Eric Blair (George Orwell) (1903–50)

George Orwell was the pen-name of Eric Blair who had done his best to purge himself of his Eton and Indian service background by deliberately sharing the life of the poor, an experience reflected in his book, *Down and Out in Paris and London* (1933).

Orwell considered himself something of an authority on pubs, 'one of the basic institutions of English life'. He loved what he called 'the familiar reviving smell' of the fug of smoke and beer. 'In a pub', Ravelston muses in *Keep the Aspidistra Flying* (1936), 'you can meet the working class on equal terms – or that's the theory anyway.' Drinking beer, or draught stout if it was available, was an essential component of Orwell's working-class performance. He once ridiculed a BBC colleague, John Morris, for not knowing how to order beer like a working man.

He preferred his pubs to be 'uncompromisingly Victorian', with the 'solid comfortable ugliness of the nineteenth century' and the traditional divisions of public, saloon and ladies' bars and 'a bottle and jug for those who are too bashful to buy their supper beer publicly'. He loved the 'elaborate social ritual' and 'animated conversation' and lamented the fact that these were being supplanted by 'the passive drug-like pleasures of cinema and radio'.

For a drinking man Orwell could be alarmingly puritanical. The writer Rayner Heppenstall, who for a while shared a flat with him, returned one night distinctly the worse for wear to be confronted with a marked absence of sympathy: 'Bit thick you know . . . This time of night . . . Wake the whole street.' When Heppenstall protested Orwell knocked him down and locked him up for the night. Heppenstall tried to kick the door down and Orwell burst in and attacked him with his shooting-stick.

The pubs of Fitzrovia, where run-down Bohemia rubbed shoulders with the working-class locals, were his regular haunt during the time he worked as a talks producer for the Overseas Department of the BBC nearby in Oxford Street. It was Orwell who was credited with initiating the move away from the Fitzroy Tavern to the smaller and more peaceful Wheatsheaf. By this time he was famous as the author of *Animal Farm* (1945). He was surrounded by new friends who called him George, commented Heppenstall, 'and I saw him as a fashionable author hobnobbing'.

Unlike Dylan Thomas or Maclaren-Ross, Orwell was not a brilliant talker. He preferred to stand on the edge of the group, quietly sipping his pint, listening. According to Anthony Burgess, Winston Smith's terror of 'the worst thing in the world' in *Nineteen Eighty-Four* (1949) owed its origin to Orwell's hearing the painter Gilbert Wood enlarging on his phobia about rats.

For a man whose physical appearance has been compared to Gustav Doré's drawings of Don Quixote, Orwell was a surprisingly enthusiastic eater-out in the Charlotte Street restaurants, particularly during the time he was working as literary editor of *Tribune*. For a while he favoured the Akropolis, but when a waiter objected to him removing his jacket he transferred his affections to the nearby Little Akropolis where the atmosphere was more free and easy.

ERIC BLAIR (GEORGE ORWELL), Felix H. Man, *c.*1949

Sonia Brownwell had a flat opposite the Akropolis. While she was working with Cyril Connolly at *Horizon*, Maclaren-Ross conceived a 'grand passion' for her and had to be kept out of the office. She married Orwell three months before his death. Rayner Heppenstall went to see him as he lay dying in a private room in University College Hospital, and Orwell, a socialist to the last, apologised for the grandeur.

Orwell would not have taken kindly to the idea of a formal portrait: the few images of him are mostly photographic, such as Felix Man's portrait of about 1949.

JULIAN MACLAREN-ROSS (1912–64)

❦

'I warn you. He's rather an egotist,' Anthony Powell was told before being introduced to Maclaren-Ross. This was, in fact, something of an understatement. Maclaren-Ross was one of the more memorable Fitzrovian characters of the forties and fifties, an inescapable figure in his camel overcoat, worn suede shoes, dark-green glasses, spectacular ties, never without his gold-topped malacca cane, except in times of hardship when it was exchanged for one with a knob of silver. He gave the impression of an 1890s dandy gone to seed, or, as Anthony Burgess put it, 'an Oscar Wilde with less talent but no homosexuality'. 'Why don't you try to look more sordid,' Dylan Thomas asked him, 'Sordidness, boy, that's the thing.' 'If you'd just come out of the glasshouse', Maclaren-Ross replied, 'you wouldn't want to look more sordid.'

Maclaren-Ross arrived on the Fitzrovian scene in 1943 after he had been invalided out of the army on pyschiatric grounds, having spent three weeks in detention for going absent-without-leave. In his time he had known considerable hardship, eked out a desperate existence as a vacuum-cleaner salesman and slept rough on the Embankment.

He and Dylan Thomas were brought together as writers of documentaries for Donald Taylor's Strand Films. These gave full scope to the authors' considerable powers of invention, but many of them never saw the light of day. 'What we really wanted to script were Features and together we planned, among other subjects a mystery film to be written in collaboration, entitled *The Whispering Gallery* or *The Distorting Mirror*.'

Maclaren-Ross was a writer of considerable talent and his short stories – 'Stuff to Give the Troops' and 'The Nine Men of Soho' – enjoyed something of a vogue in the forties, but an irresistible paranoia drove him into endless and tedious disputes with publishers and editors and his life-style limited his writing time to the hours between midnight and dawn.

Opening time would always find him at his jealously guarded post in the Wheatsheaf, where he would remain until the afternoon. The hours between then and evening opening would pass in a leisurely examination of the bookshops on the Charing Cross Road and he would be back at his corner of the bar by six o'clock. At closing time there would be the customary dash down to the Highlander in Soho and then he would return

JULIAN MACLAREN-ROSS, unknown photographer, *c.*1950

to the Scala restaurant in Charlotte Street, taking the last underground train from Goodge Street to one of the mysterious and shabby hotels where he lodged.

And all this time he talked. He was the most relentless of the Fitzrovian monologists. 'He was arrogant and exacting in company', Dan Davin wrote in his memoirs (*Closing Times*, 1975). 'He did not like to take his share in conversation; or rather, when he took his turn he did not let it go. To those who were not prepared to let him have the lion's share of the conversation, he seemed a pretentious bore.'

Maclaren-Ross's anecdotes were endlessly repeated, acquiring polish and point at each retelling. Much of his talk was of books and writers. He had an almost total recall of the details of any book published in his lifetime and an equally encyclopaedic knowledge of the cinema, particularly gangster films. Anthony Powell said that whenever Maclaren-Ross began to give his impersonation of Sydney Greenstreet, it was time to depart. Although he seemed to be able to consume limitless amounts of alcohol without visible effect, there came a stage in the evening when loquacity would be overtaken by irritability. There would be angry words with barmen and cab drivers, and the police might be called in – 'Take that man's number, Constable.' The proceedings would invariably backfire.

'For a while', wrote Anthony Powell, 'he walked his own unique tightrope above the by-ways of Charlotte Street . . . his gifts as a writer never quite allowing the headlong descent forever threatened by his behaviour as a man.' Maclaren-Ross was always about to commit to paper the book that was to be his masterpiece, 'Night's Black Agents', but never got round to writing it. Thanks to the efforts of R. D. Smith of the BBC he supported himself in the late fifties by a series of radio thrillers, presented in his fine handwriting. He disdained the typewriter, preferring always his Parker pen, known as the Hooded Terror. He died celebrating an unexpected cheque for a radio repeat, rather in the fashion of his *alter ego*, X. Trapnel in *A Dance to the Music of Time*.

Portraits of Maclaren-Ross are non-existent, and even photographs are rare; the image shown on the previous page must be the only one to show him without his dark glasses.

JAMES MEARY TAMBIMUTTU (1915–83)

Tambimuttu, the 'wild dark impresario of the dithering forties', burst upon the Fitzrovian scene on the eve of the Second World War. He came from Sri Lanka, and with his blue-black hair and flashing eyes reminded the critic Derek Stanford of the 'damsel with a dulcimer' in 'Kubla Khan'.

The poet Kathleen Raine compared him to Dionysus: '"I love ecstasy", I remember him saying, and with Tambi ecstasy, with or without the help of the soma, never seemed to flag.' All editors of little magazines see their publications as beacons in a dark world, and Tambimuttu was no exception. In *Poetry London*, which he set up with Dylan Thomas, and which survived from 1939 until 1947, he pioneered work by Stephen Spender, Louis MacNeice, David Gascoyne, George Barker, Gavin Ewart and, perceptively, the young Harold Pinter. Henry Moore, Mervyn Peake and Ceri Richards were persuaded to provide decorations.

Eccentric Tambimuttu was, in the best Fitzrovian tradition. His editorial headquarters ranged from the steam room of the Russell Square public baths to the Hog in the Pound in Oxford Street, and when all else failed he would set himself up in a damp basement. Lawrence Durrell arrived to find 'that the entire contents of his first number reposed under his bed in an enormous Victorian chamber pot. It was into this he dipped for his authors.'

Practicality was not always his strongest suit. When Muriel Spark was obliged to leave the Poetry Society, Tambimuttu's response was characteristically utopian:

> *He began by saying that he had heard that during Mrs Spark's editorship the resources of the Society had fallen gravely. That was very good: that was how things should be. A poetry society ought to be for poets, not shopkeepers or stockbrokers. Poets needed money, very badly indeed. Shopkeepers and stockbrokers did* not *need money. They had plenty of it already. If you paid your poets well, your funds would sink. That was a proof you were doing your job.*

(Derek Stanford, *Inside the Forties*, 1977)

Julian Maclaren-Ross recounted a story of a girl coming down from Oxford to work as Tambimuttu's secretary:

'Do you have any money?'
'Yes, thank you. I've got £5.'
'That is good,' Tambi said. *'I am a Prince in my country and princes don't carry money, you know. Give me the fiver and later the firm will refund you. I am going to lunch with T. S. Eliot. You know who is T. S. Eliot?'*
'Yes indeed.'
Tambi stowed away the fiver. *'He takes interest in me and in the quarterly,'* he said.

(Julian Maclaren-Ross, *Memoirs of the Forties*, 1965)

JAMES MEARY TAMBIMUTTU, unknown photographer, n.d.

The last was perfectly true. It was Eliot who had helped him get *Poetry London* off the ground. He described Tambimuttu as 'the most courageous of the younger publishers'. 'He is really a wild man like me', was Tambimuttu's unexpected response.

It was Tambimuttu who memorably introduced Maclaren-Ross to the Fitzrovian scene in 1943 and warned him to beware.

> *'It is a dangerous place, you must be careful.'*
> *'Fights with knives?'*
> *'No, a worse danger. You might get Sohoitis, you know.'*
> *'No I don't. What is it?'*
> *'If you get Sohoitis,' Tambi said very seriously, 'you will stay there always day and night and get no work done ever. You have been warned.'*

Tambimuttu was regarded by the literary world with a mesmerised affection. He could be exasperating, he frequently lost manuscripts and was adept at manipulating poets into buying him lunch. He seemed always on the edge of disaster and always fell on his feet. His patrons included several American millionairesses, the Beatles and Mrs Gandhi.

ANTHONY POWELL (BORN 1905)

Anthony Powell recorded his impressions of Fitzrovia in his autobiography, *To Keep the Ball Rolling*. In 1926 he had taken a job at Gerald Duckworth & Co. in Henrietta Street, Covent Garden, to 'learn the business of publishing'. One of the books in preparation there was Osbert Sitwell's *The People's Album of London Statues*, for which Nina Hamnett was supplying the illustrations. Powell met her when she came in to deliver them. She suggested that she should draw his portrait, and one thing led to another, as it generally did with Nina, and they became lovers. She called him her 'little Etonian'. The poet and historian Peter Quennell told her biographer, Denise Hooker, that Powell was 'rather pleased with it at the time. He built her up as a romantic *femme de trente ans*, a Bohemian mistress.'

ANTHONY POWELL,
H. (Hubert) Andrew
Freeth, n.d.

Powell was introduced to Fitzrovia's drinking haunts, 'really pubs, not smartened up into the pseudo cocktail lounges they have since become', and to some of their more remarkable customers. Betty May he already knew, since Duckworth published her autobiography: 'With her hair tied up in a coloured handkerchief, she would not have been out of place telling fortunes at a fair.' Tommy Earp told Powell of the time when, in an alcoholic stupor, he had taken refuge under the tarpaulin cover of a Covent Garden barrow and woken up the following morning in a distant part of London.

Powell drew on his Fitzrovia experiences for his novel sequence *A Dance to the Music of Time* (1951–75), and many of its characters are reflected fleetingly there. Something of Augustus John can be glimpsed in Isbister; some of Philip Heseltine's musical opinions and certainly the manner of his suicide were borrowed for Maclintick; and Dr Trelawny proclaiming 'The Essence of the All is the Godhead of the Truth' owes more than a little to Aleister Crowley.

Powell would only admit to two portraits. The first was Constant Lambert:

> *Moreland, musician, wit, sometimes exuberant, sometimes melancholy, has the Bronzino features already described as Lambert's. There the resemblance fades, invention, imagination – whatever you like to call it – takes over. If I have been skilful enough to pass on any of Lambert's incomparable wit, then Moreland is like him . . .*

The other was Maclaren-Ross, who figures memorably and very recognisably as X. Trapnel, the lover of Widmerpool's wife Pamela, who destroys both him and his masterpiece, *Profiles in String*. Powell disguised him with a beard, transformed his malacca cane into a swordstick tipped with a death's head and substituted mention of Boris Karloff for Sydney Greenstreet as 'a signal that a late evening must be brought resolutely to a close'.

One cannot help thinking that Maclaren-Ross, who took such pride in his detailed knowledge of the novel in his own time, might have been pleased. He would certainly have talked about it, endlessly.

OSBERT, EDITH AND SACHEVERELL SITWELL, Cecil Beaton, 1927

Edith Sitwell (1887–1964), Osbert Sitwell (1892–1969) and Sacheverell Sitwell (1897–1988)

The Sitwells make rather unlikely Fitzrovians. It is difficult to imagine Edith sitting in the Wheatsheaf helping out Mrs Stewart with her crossword, or Sacheverell holding the ladder for Charlie Allchild as he extracted money-laden darts from the ceiling of the Fitzroy. Yet the Sitwells hover over Fitzrovia like Olympians in a Thornhill ceiling, bestowing their blessing and their patronage. Their myth-making potential was captured and exploited in the photographs of Cecil Beaton.

It was Edith who led the way, taking Osbert to have tea with Sickert in his Fitzroy Street studio, and it was Edith who first got to know Nina Hamnett (who painted Osbert's portrait), 'one of the most generous people one could imagine'. Nina introduced Edith to the keeper of the Ethnographical Department of the British Museum and to the African masks that were to figure in the most socially aware of all her poems, 'Gold Coast Customs' (1929).

The focal point of the Sitwells' Fitzrovia was the Tour Eiffel restaurant, where, despite the astronomical prices and the indifferent food, Osbert entertained his friends. It was here that they celebrated after a performance of *Façade* at the Chenil Galleries, with William Walton, Lambert, Cecil Beaton, Nina Hamnett and Jack Lindsay, where they encountered Tallulah Bankhead and watched Augustus John 'making grabs at some silly little idiots dressed up as Sapphists'.

Lambert was on easy terms with all the Sitwells and took them in his stride. He had made Osbert's acquaintance by turning up on his doorstep and ringing the bell; he had set several of Sacheverell's poems to music before scoring his public triumph with 'The Rio Grand' (1928). He had even, on a visit to Renishaw, encountered their father, Sir George, crawling through the garden on his hands and knees with a malacca walking-stick in his mouth.

Dylan Thomas was Edith's most celebrated Fitzrovian conquest. 'Can you tell me about Miss S?' he asked Robert Herring, 'She isn't very frightening is she?' When the broadcaster Wynford Vaughan Thomas, a

OSBERT SITWELL, Nina Hamnett, *c*.1918

great supporter of the Fitzroy, asked her how Thomas had behaved at their first meeting, she replied, 'Beautifully, I've never seen him behave anything but beautifully. He always behaved with me like a son with his mother.'

Edith found work for Thomas, tried to secure him a grant from the Royal Literary Fund and pressed for a travelling scholarship to take him abroad – 'We are not likely to get another man of such genius'. Thomas was always rather guarded about speaking of her verse, but he was in no doubt about the central importance of poetry in her life: 'If poetry was taken away from Edith she mightn't die, but she'd be bloody sick.'

The Fitzrovian who did praise her verse with intelligence and insight was the communist poet Jack Lindsay, the one-time lover of Betty May. He did, admittedly, try to hijack her poems for the Marxist cause, but this did not dampen her gratitude: 'You understand what was in my mind when I wrote "The Shadow of Cain"' she told him, 'in a manner so extraordinary that you might have been the poem's author.'

Edward Alexander 'Aleister' Crowley
(1875–1947)

The Fitzrovians were in two minds about Aleister Crowley, the self-styled 'Great Beast', '666', 'Baphomet' and, according to the magazine *John Bull*, 'A Man We'd Like to Hang'. Nina Hamnett, who counted herself a friend of his until he sued her for libel, was a member of his Order of the Silver Star, an occult society which performed the Eleusinian mysteries at the Caxton Hall. Jack Lindsay wrote him off as a fraud; Anthony Powell thought he had the manner of 'an old music-hall comedian', but was convinced that he was 'intensely sinister' both in appearance and manner. Dylan Thomas was sitting in a pub drawing doodles at a table when Crowley walked over from the other side of the room and presented him with an exact replica of his doodle.

Crowley believed, or said that he believed, that he had been born many times. His previous incarnations included the Borgia pope Alexander VI, the Elizabethan necromancer Edmund Kelley and the magician Cagliostro. His own birth was rather less spectacular. He was born in Leamington Spa, the son of a brewer who was a fanatical member of the Plymouth Brethren. At Trinity College, Cambridge, he studied moral sciences but developed a passion for mountain climbing – in the Alps, in Mexico and in the Himalayas where he made an unsuccessful attempt on Kanchenjunga. In 1898 he became a member of the occult Society of the Golden Dawn, admitted as Brother Perdurabo, and for the rest of his life was a determined prophet and practitioner of the black arts. Very soon the most fantastic stories, many of them concocted by himself, began to spread: he had transformed the poet Victor Neuberg into a camel and put him in the zoo at Algiers, he and one of his disciples had raised the god Pan in a Left Bank hotel and in the morning the disciple was found dead. If any of his enemies met with a sudden death, Crowley was inevitably credited with causing it; when Nina Hamnett died, Crowley was, in some obscure way, held to be responsible.

Although Crowley's pursuit of the magic mysteries was undoubtedly a deadly serious affair, there was something of the joker and mountebank about him. 'Like many Englishmen,' wrote his friend the biographer and novelist Louis Wilkinson, 'he had in some ways never grown up.' Under

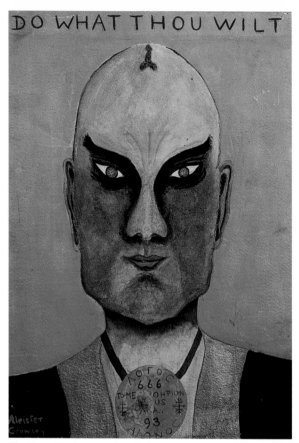

The Master Therion 666, Edward Alexander 'Aleister' Crowley, self-portrait, 1918

the alias of Lord Boleskine Crowley took a house on the shores of Loch Ness where he led a Swiss visitor off on a hunt for the Haggis, which was, he assured him, a sacred and taboo animal. Nor was he above using his magical operation for gain. He noted with satisfaction after one of his occult operations that Consols (Consolidated Annuities) had risen from $71\frac{1}{2}$ to $76\frac{1}{4}$ points.

Crowley's pursuit of his craft took him to China and to the deserts of North Africa. He employed alcohol, sex and all manner of drugs – opium, heroine, cocaine – as gateways to his excursions into the astral plane. Inevitably he left behind him a trail of destruction, disciples, wives, and the 'scarlet women' who assisted him in his conjurations were likely to end up insane or alcoholic or both.

Crowley once proclaimed himself the greatest living English poet and, in fact, three of his verses did find their way into the *Oxford Book of Mystical Verse*. At his funeral in Brighton, Louis Wilkinson recited his 'Hymn to Pan':

And I rave; and I rage and I rip and I rend
Everlasting, world without end.

At the next meeting of Brighton Corporation it was resolved that 'no such pagan or blasphemous ceremony . . . should ever again be permitted within this jurisdiction.'

Something of the complexity of Crowley's personality is borne out by the two portraits reproduced here – the self-portrait in which he resembles one of his own demons, and the rather wistful, tweedy character caught by Augustus John.

EDWARD ALEXANDER 'ALEISTER' CROWLEY, Augustus John, *c*.1914

NANCY CUNARD (1896–1965)
🍃

'Everybody old, it is hoped,' wrote Raymond Mortimer, 'can look back to one person who was incomparably bewitching, and I have never met anyone to equal Nancy Cunard when I first met her.' In 1911 Nancy Cunard and Iris Tree, the daughter of the celebrated actor-manager Beerbohm Tree, rented a studio in Fitzroy Place, at the end of Charlotte Street. Nancy's mother, the American-born Lady Cunard, had bolted from her husband, Sir Bache, and the Gothic splendours of Nevill Holt, to pursue her passionate love affair with the conductor Thomas Beecham, and Nancy was making her own attempt to assert her independence. Her escapade came to an end all too soon when she and Iris Tree were arrested for swimming in the Serpentine in the small hours of the morning, and she was taken back under her mother's wing.

Marriage proved a more effective way of escaping from her mother's circle, but by 1919 her brief union with Sydney Fairbairn was over and she decided to settle in Paris. For her London base, she chose the Tour Eiffel in Percy Street; there she could drink with Augustus John, Nina Hamnett, Osbert Sitwell, Ezra Pound and Tommy Earp, secure in the knowledge that it was one place where she was never likely to meet her mother. It was at the Tour Eiffel that she met the Armenian novelist Dikran Kovyoumdjian, better known by his more accessible pen-name, Michael Arlen. They became lovers – Nancy's friends invariably did – and she figured in his novels, notably as Iris March in *The Green Hat* (1924): 'She was of all time. She was, when the first woman crawled out of the mud of the primeval world. She would be, when the last woman walks to the unmentionable end.'

Nancy was portrayed in rather less extravagant terms by another of her lovers, Aldous Huxley, in *Those Barren Leaves* (1925) and *Point Counterpoint* (1928), and most memorably in *Antic Hay* (1923) as Mrs Viveash: 'Her elbows propped on the mantelpiece, her chin resting on her clasped hands, she was looking fixedly at her own image in the glass. Pale eyes looked unwaveringly into pale eyes. The red mouth and its reflection exchanged their smiles of pain.' With her piercing eyes, her voice which seemed always on the point of dying away, her painfully thin arms, adorned, as in Beaton's photograph, with African bracelets, Nancy Cunard became a twenties icon. She was rarely sober, but never entirely drunk, she took lovers as casually

NANCY CUNARD, Cecil Beaton, late 1920s

and as indiscriminately as Nina Hamnett and could be alarmingly predatory. She was photographed by Man Ray and painted by Kokoschka. The French Surrealist poet Louis Aragon joined the list of her lovers and converted her to Marxism.

It was not until 1927 that Nancy discovered her real *métier*. She acquired an old hand-printing press and at a Normandy farmhouse – Les Puits Carré at La Chapelle Reanville – she set up the Hours Press, publishing work by Ezra Pound, Robert Graves, Harold Acton, Aragon's translation of Lewis Carroll's 'The Hunting of the Snark' and poems by the young Samuel Beckett.

Her assistant at the Press was Henry Crowder, a black American jazz pianist whom Nancy had 'acquired' in Venice. When Lady Cunard got to hear of him she was so outraged that Beecham wrote to Nancy to warn her of the danger of bringing Crowder to England. When Nancy installed herself and her lover in the Tour Eiffel, the hotel was so plagued with police and private detectives sent by her ladyship that the proprietor, Stulik, begged her to leave.

Nancy took up the cause of black rights with passionate zeal, and from a room in Percy Street she canvassed writers all over the world for contributions to a vast anthology, *Negro*, 'for the recording of the struggles and achievements, the persecutions and the revolt against them of the Negro peoples'. It was published in 1934 and dedicated to Crowder.

The book – eight hundred pages of it – emphatically marked the end of Nancy's days as a social butterfly and the beginning of her career of social and political protest. As she grew older she became wilder and more fanatical, drunker and sexually voracious, plunging steadily into paranoia. She was arrested in London for soliciting and was certified as insane. Through her own determination and the loyalty of her friends she recovered and was released to return to France, where she died in 1965.

MALCOLM LOWRY (1909–57)

It was, perhaps, inevitable that the most legendary of self-destructive drinkers, the novelist and poet Malcolm Lowry, should settle briefly in Fitzrovia. In 1932, having already blazed an alcoholic trail through Boston with his friend and mentor, the poet Conrad Aiken, he managed to persuade his father to allow him to spend some time in London while he was trying to find a publisher for his first novel, *Ultramarine* (1933). It had been stipulated that he should stay at a temperance hotel, the Kenilworth, in Great Russell Street, close to the British Museum, but Lowry soon found himself lodgings in Old Gloucester Street, passing his days with what John Davenport, a friend from Lowry's Cambridge days, described as 'the sad detritus of humanity that haunts London's Quartier Latin'.

In *Under the Volcano* (1947), the novel that was to bring Lowry 'an absolutely obscene success', Hugh recollects his meeting with a luckless hot-dog seller:

> *How could he expect to sell anything so revolutionary as a hot dog in Oxford Street? He might as well try ice-cream at the South Pole. No, the idea was to camp outside a pub down a back alley, and that not any pub, but the Fitzroy Tavern in Charlotte Street, chock full of starving artists drinking themselves to death simply because their souls pined away, each night between eight and ten, for lack of just such a thing as a hot dog. That was the place to go!*

MALCOLM LOWRY, Clarissa Aiken, 1929

Lowry soon became a familiar figure in the Fitzroy and in all the neighbouring pubs, playing jazz and spirituals on his ukulele, getting epically drunk with the writer Robert Pocock (then pursuing a rather incongruous career as a policeman), and giving advice and encouragement to the young Dylan Thomas. Like many of the other Fitzrovians

MALCOLM LOWRY, unknown photographer, n.d.

he found his way to 'La Tour Bourgeoise', the Parliament Hill house of the poet Anna Wickham – 'I may be a minor poet but I'm a major woman' – who wrote for him a little epitaph which did not call for much prophetic skill: 'You'll sink/ Through drink.'

Lowry continued to haunt the bars and cafés of London's Bohemia until the end of 1934, pursuing the woman who was to be his first wife, Jan Gabrial, felling a cart-horse by punching it on the jaw and astonishing his former tutor, Hugh Sykes Davies (another of Betty May's lovers) by pouring eau de Cologne into his shoes: 'I notice that the hot weather makes my feet smell.'

Lowry departed for his long self-imposed exile in France, New York, Mexico and Vancouver, returning to England in 1954. All his life he battled to give up alcohol always returning to the same point: 'The only hope is the next drink.' Even when he did manage to give up for a while some chance event or disaster – a trip to a pub with Robert Pocock or the death of Dylan Thomas – would send him back again. He died, or may have taken his own life, in Ripe, in Sussex in 1957.

LIST OF ILLUSTRATIONS

Map of Fitzrovia
© National Portrait Gallery

Henry Fuseli, 1741–1825
James Northcote, 1778
Oil on canvas, feigned
incomplete oval,
77.8 x 64.5 cm
© National Portrait Gallery
(5469)

John Constable, 1776–1837
Self-portrait, c.1804
Pencil and chalk,
24.8 x 19.4 cm
© National Portrait Gallery
(901)

The Fitzroy Tavern
Charles Allchild, 1930s
Modern print, 16.5 x 10.8 cm
© Sally Fiber

Drinking at the Fitzroy Tavern
Unknown photographer, 1930s
Modern print, 10.8 x 16 cm
© Sally Fiber

Walter Sickert, 1860–1942
Philip Wilson Steer, before
1894
Oil on canvas, 59.7 x 29.8 cm
© Reserved
National Portrait Gallery
(3142)

Walter Sickert, 1860–1942
Edmond Xavier Kapp, 1940
Pen and ink, 31.4 x 20 cm
© Estate of Edmond Xavier
Kapp
National Portrait Gallery
(3547)

Nina Hamnett, 1890–1956
Walter Sickert, c.1916
Pencil and pen and ink on
brown paper, 25.5 x 19 cm
The Estate of Walter Sickert,
All Rights Reserved, DACS,
1999
Photograph © Courtesy
Sotheby's, London

Nina Hamnett, 1890–1956
Daniel Farson, 1952
Bromide print, 17.5 x 17.4 cm
© National Portrait Gallery
(P288)

Augustus John, 1878–1961
Sir William Orpen, exhibited
1900
Oil on canvas, 99.1 x 94 cm
By courtesy of the Estate of Sir
William Orpen/National
Portrait Gallery (4252)

Augustus John, 1878–1961
?John Hope-Johnson, n.d.
Snapshot print, 8.7 x 6.7 cm
© National Portrait Gallery
(Ax13021)

Lady Ottoline Morrell,
1873–1938
Augustus John, 1919
Oil on canvas, 69 x 51.1 cm
© Julius White
National Portrait Gallery (6095)

Augustus John, 1878–1961
Bill Brandt, before 1946
Bromide print, 25.1 x 19.7 cm
Bill Brandt © Bill Brandt
Archive Ltd
National Portrait Gallery (P191)

Percy Wyndham Lewis,
1882–1957
Self-portrait, 1932
Ink and wash, 25.4 x 19.7 cm
© Estate of Mrs G.A. Wyndham
Lewis
National Portrait Gallery (4528)

Percy Wyndham Lewis,
1882–1957
Michael Ayrton, 1955
Conté crayon, 62.9 x 50.5 cm
© Estate of Michael Ayrton
National Portrait Gallery (5995)

Dylan Thomas, 1914–53
Augustus John, c.1937–8
Oil on canvas, 45.7 x 33.7 cm
© Julius White
National Portrait Gallery (L213)

Dylan Thomas, 1914–53
Michael Ayrton, 1945
Charcoal, 39.4 x 29.8 cm
© Estate of Michael Ayrton
National Portrait Gallery (4089)

Betty May, 1901–58
Nina Hamnett, n.d.
Pen and ink
© The Estate of Nina Hamnett

Constant Lambert, 1905–51
Christopher Wood, 1926
Oil on canvas, 91.4 x 55.9 cm
© National Portrait Gallery
(4443)

Margot Fonteyn, 1919–91 (in
Horoscope)
Gordon Anthony, 1938
Modern print, 24 x 18.5 cm
V&A Picture Library
(BW56409)

Alan Rawsthorne, 1905–71
Isabel Rawsthorne, 1966
Oil on canvas, 65.8 x 81.3 cm
© National Portrait Gallery
(6175)

Alan Rawsthorne, 1905–71
Cecil Beaton, 1948
Semi-matte bromide print,
24.4 x 19.4 cm
© Courtesy Sotheby's, London
National Portrait Gallery
(x14186)

An excerpt from 'First
Rhapsody', E. J. Moeran, 1928
Modern print, 10.9 x 16.7 cm
© Sally Fiber

E. J. Moeran, 1894–1950
Augustus John, c.1927
Pen and ink, 24.5 x 16.5 cm
© Julius White
Photograph © Phillips

E. J. Moeran, 1894–1950
Howard Coster, 1944
Modern print, 19.2 x 14.2 cm
© National Portrait Gallery
(x23787)